Pebble®

FAMOUS
ATHLETES

CRISTIANO
RONALDO

by Mari Schuh

CAPSTONE PRESS
a capstone imprint

Pebble Plus is published by Capstone Press,
1710 Roe Crest Drive, North Mankato, Minnesota 56003
www.capstonepub.com

Library of Congress Cataloging-in-Publication Data
Schuh, Mari C., 1975-
  Cristiano Ronaldo / by Mari Schuh.
    pages cm. — (Pebble Plus. Famous Athletes)
  Includes webography.
  Includes bibliographical references and index.
  Summary: "Presents the life of professional soccer athlete Cristiano Ronaldo in an
introductory biography with a timeline and photos"— Provided by publisher.
  ISBN 978-1-4914-8508-8 (library binding)
  ISBN 978-1-4914-8528-6 (paperback)
  ISBN 978-1-4914-8524-8 (eBook PDF)
  1. Ronaldo, Cristiano, 1985-—Juvenile literature. 2. Soccer players—Portugal—
Biography—Juvenile literature. I. Title.
  GV942.7.R626S38 2016
  796.334092—dc23
  [B]   2015021178

Note to Parents and Teachers

The Famous Athletes supports national curriculum standards for
social studies related to people, places, and culture. This book
describes and illustrates Cristiano Ronaldo. The images support
early readers in understanding the text. The repetition of words
and phrases helps early readers learn new words. This book also
introduces early readers to subject-specific vocabulary words,
which are defined in the Glossary section. Early readers may need
assistance to read some words and to use the Table of Contents,
Glossary, Read More, Internet Sites, and Index sections of the book.

Printed and bound in the United States.
009368CGS16

TABLE OF CONTENTS

1985

born in
Funchal,
Portugal

EARLY LIFE

Soccer star Cristiano Ronaldo was born February 5, 1985. At age 8, he played for a small soccer club. His dad was the club's equipment manager.

1985

born in
Funchal,
Portugal

6

As a boy, Cristiano loved
to play soccer. By age 10, he
was becoming a young star.
He played for youth soccer teams
in Portugal for many years.

1985

born in
Funchal,
Portugal

TOP SCORER

In 2002 Cristiano played

on Sporting Lisbon's main team.

He scored two goals in his first game.

His skills made him a great forward.

Forwards try to score goals.

1985

2003

born in
Funchal,
Portugal

starts to
play for
Manchester
United in
England

SOCCER SUPERSTAR

Cristiano worked hard to be one

of the best. He was strong and fast.

He could kick goals with either foot.

Soon, he was one of the best

forwards in soccer.

1985
born in
Funchal,
Portugal

2003
starts to
play for
Manchester
United in
England

2008
wins his first
Ballon d'Or
award

Cristiano had a great year in 2008. He helped Manchester United win three championships. Cristiano also won the Ballon d'Or award. It is given to the world's best soccer player.

1985
born in
Funchal,
Portugal

2003
starts to
play for
Manchester
United in
England

2008
wins his first
Ballon d'Or
award

In 2009 Cristiano started to play for Real Madrid. He became the most expensive soccer player. The next season, he set a team scoring record. He scored 53 goals.

2009

starts to play
for Real
Madrid in
Spain

1985

born in
Funchal,
Portugal

2003

starts to
play for
Manchester
United in
England

2008

wins his first
Ballon d'Or
award

Cristiano has won many awards.

He won the Ballon d'Or award again

in 2013 and 2014. Cristiano has also been

named World Soccer Player

of the Year three times.

starts to play
for Real
Madrid in
Spain

wins
Ballon d'Or
award

1985
born in Funchal, Portugal

2003
starts to play for Manchester United in England

2008
wins his first Ballon d'Or award

In 2015 Cristiano scored his 300th goal for Real Madrid. He is one of the best soccer players in the world today. He also may be one of the best in history.

starts to play for Real Madrid in Spain

wins Ballon d'Or award

scores 300th goal for Real Madrid

GLOSSARY

Ballon d'Or—an award given each year to the best soccer player in the world; Ballon d'Or means golden ball

championship—a contest or tournament that decides which team is the best

expensive—costing a lot of money

forward—a player whose main job is to score goals

international—including more than one nation

World Cup—a soccer competition held every four years in a different country; teams from around the world compete against each other

CRITICAL THINKING
USING THE COMMON CORE

1. How was Cristiano's dad involved in soccer? How might have this helped Cristiano become a soccer star? (Key Ideas and Details)

2. What is the name of an award Cristiano has won? Why might have he been given this award? (Integration of Knowledge and Ideas)

3. How did Cristiano help his team win soccer games? Why is this important? (Integration of Knowledge and Ideas)

READ MORE

Lindeen, Mary. *Let's Play Soccer!* Chicago: Norwood House Press, 2015.

Morey, Allan. *Soccer.* Minneapolis, Minn.: Jump!, 2015.

Nagelhout, Ryan. *I Love Soccer.* New York: Gareth Stevens Publishing, 2015.

Nelson, Robin. *Soccer Is Fun!* Minneapolis, Minn.: Lerner Publications, 2014.

INTERNET SITES

FactHound offers a safe, fun way to find Internet sites related to this book. All of the sites on FactHound have been researched by our staff.

Here's all you do:

Visit *www.facthound.com*

Type in this code: 9781491485088

Super-cool stuff!

Check out projects, games and lots more at
www.capstonekids.com

INDEX

Editorial Credits
Gina Kammer, editor; Juliette Peters, designer;
Eric Gohl, media researcher; Lori Barbeau, production specialist

Photo Credits
Getty Images: AFP/Antonio Cotrim, 8, VI Images, 4, 6; Newscom: Reuters/Ian
Hodgson, 10, Reuters/Nigel Roddis, 14, SIPA/Olympia/Galimberti, 12, ZUMA
Press/Juan Aguado, 20; Shutterstock: AGIF, 18, Marcos Mesa Sam Wordley,
cover, 1, Natursports, 16

Design Elements: Shutterstock